Our First Bus Ride

Our First Bus Ride

Written by: Derek Francis
Illustrated by: Ashley Finch

OUR FIRST BUS RIDE

Written by Derek Francis
Illustrated by Ashley Finch
Book Design by Jermaine Taris

Printed in the USA
First Printing 2026

Published by Strive Publishing LLC, Minneapolis, MN
www.strivepubandco.com

ISBN 978-1-948529-26-6 (Hardcover)
Library of Congress Control Number: 2025927498

STRIVE
Publishing · Bookstore
BREAKING BARRIERS BOOK BY BOOK

www.strivepubandco.com

This book is dedicated to my daughter, Grace and all students in schools, to find joy in the gift of building friendships in schools and the community with getting to know people of different backgrounds.

One Fall morning in Minneapolis, two girls stepped onto a yellow school bus.

It looked like a regular bus ride.

But it wasn't.

Monica and Molly remember being part of something important called integration.

Integration means bringing children from different schools and different races together, so everyone is treated fairly.

This was not just a bus ride.

It was a step toward fairness.

Monica's curls bounced as she skated beside her best friend, Molly. Molly's big laugh echoed down the sidewalk.

"Are you ready to go roller skating?" Monica called.

The girls zoomed past their yards, giggling, full of energy and excitement—just two friends enjoying a spring day in the neighborhood.

One afternoon, a neighbor waved them over.
Her golden retriever had just had puppies!

"PUPPIES!" they both shouted, dropping their backpacks. The neighbor beamed as Monica and Molly cuddled the soft, wiggly pups on the grass.

"Would you girls like to take one home?" she asked.

That evening, both girls asked their
parents the same question:

"Can I have a puppy?"

Molly's parents said yes.
She named her new pup Honey.

Monica's mom sighed, "We just don't
have enough space or time right now."

Monica understood, and she knew she could
have fun with Molly and her puppy anyway.

Every morning, Monica and Molly walked to Field School together past Mrs. Johnson's rose bushes, under tall elm trees, and over bumpy sidewalk cracks.

They made up songs about homework, guessed what was in each other's lunch bags, and sometimes made funny faces at squirrels along the way.

As the school year came to an end, Ms. Ellis, their first-grade teacher told them that some big changes were coming for second grade.

Lesson time with
Ms. Ellis
1954 Brown VS B.O.E.
Little Rock 9
1957
Ruby
Bridges
1960
Hale-Field
1971

Ms. Ellis said, “For next school year our school will be a part of a program called the Hale-Field Pairing.”

She went on to explain that there were some parts of Minneapolis where white children and Black children go to separate schools.

The schools with mostly Black children were not getting the same resources as the schools where all the children were white, and that was not fair. It was also against our country’s law.

Ms. Ellis asked the students, “Has anyone heard about the Little Rock Nine? They were the first Black students to go to a high school in Arkansas where all the students were white.”

Then she asked, “Has anyone heard of Ruby Bridges? She was six years old when she helped integrate schools in New Orleans.”

Hale-Field
Pairing

"Just like the Little Rock Nine and Ruby Bridges helped make schools fair, you will help integrate schools in Minneapolis," Ms. Ellis said.

"Hale School has big classrooms, a full library, and a huge playground," she explained.

"Field School doesn't have all of that yet. So, our community planned the Hale-Field Pairing."

"All kindergarten through third graders will go to Hale School, and fourth through sixth graders will go to Field School. Both schools will get great teachers, books, and fun new classes like music, cooking, and carpentry."

Monica raised her hand.
"Will Molly and I still be together?"

"Yes!" said Ms. Ellis.

NO PAIRING!
STOP SPENDY WENDY
NO BUSING!!!
QUALITY EDUCATION FOR ALL BUT NO BUSING!!
NO BUS!
NO PAIRING!
NO BUS!

In Minneapolis not everyone liked the idea
of pairing Hale School and Field School.
Some Hale School families protested
and rallied against the pairing.

People carried large signs that said, “no pairing,”
and “no busing.” Instead of being a part of the
pairing, some Hale School families moved to the
suburbs or sent their children to private schools.

Even after all the protesting, the
Hale-Field pairing was set to begin.

Monica and Molly were excited for their first bus ride and first day at Hale School. They both couldn't wait.

For the first day of school, Monica's mom straightened her hair and trimmed her bangs and bought her a colorful outfit with flowers.

Molly's mom sewed her a new dress and her grandma bought her shiny new shoes.

Both girls felt nervous—but excited too.

STOP

That first morning at the bus stop, children had their name tags on and held their lunch boxes.

Monica and Molly waited in line together as butterflies fluttered in their stomachs. There were news cameras and reporters standing by, ready to capture the historic first bus ride to begin the Hale-Field Pairing.

The yellow bus pulled up with a *roar*. Monica and Molly climbed on and sat together near the front of the bus.

HALE
SCHOOL

In other parts of the country, the first day of bringing Black students into a school with all white students was sometimes met with shouting and protests. But the first day at Hale School was different.

When the buses pulled up to Hale, families and community members stood outside watching with excitement. Teachers and school helpers were there too, smiling warmly as they welcomed each child.

This was a big moment—not just for Monica and Molly, but for the city of Minneapolis.

HALE

Inside Hale School, their eyes grew wide.
"Whoa!" said Molly. "This hallway is huge!"

"Look at the playground!" Monica pointed.

"The library has carpet!" they both exclaimed.
There were brand-new books and fun classes.

The teachers were welcoming, and the
school felt like a whole new world.

Over at Field School, almost everyone knew Mr. Andrews. He was a kind, caring Black teacher with a big smile and an even bigger heart.

Over the years, Mr. Andrews was a teacher, a principal, and a coach— a grown-up who always knew how to cheer kids on. He grew up in Alabama where he marched with Martin Luther King Jr. for civil rights.

In his wood shop class, students used real tools on all kinds of projects including fixing chairs and tables.

Students liked Mr. Andrews because he made everyone feel welcomed and seen.

DINOS

That year, students from both schools read stories from many cultures, took field trips, and made new friends. The students didn't just learn reading and math—they began exploring new kinds of learning too!

They could discover their own special talents in fun "option classes." Some students learned to take pictures with real cameras. Others tried using computers for the very first time.

There were classes for cooking tasty foods, making music, and learning new languages. They also went on field trips to explore community events and museums.

Monica and Molly would share many more bus rides to school together, but a picture from their first bus ride was shared in the local newspaper! That picture let people in the city know what that first day was like for them.

They would always remember that morning, sitting side by side on one of the first buses to bring Black children to a school that had all white students. That first bus ride wasn't just a trip to school. It was a big moment for Hale and Field schools, and for Minnesota history!

Photo Credit: Original image from the Minneapolis Star, September 2, 1971.
Courtesy of The Minnesota Historical Society.

Prior to the Hale-Field pairing, Hale's student population was 99 percent white, while Field's was nearly 70 percent Black.

Following the pairing, both schools' enrollments shifted to approximately 30 percent students of color. What distinguished the Hale-Field Pairing from desegregation efforts in other cities was its intentional commitment to keeping both schools open.

Elsewhere, desegregation often meant closing the predominantly Black school, resulting in the loss of jobs for staff and educators.

The Hale-Field pairing helped pave the way for broader desegregation efforts across Minnesota.

Today, Monica Lash and Molly Johnson are still friends and teach their children and those in the community about how important it is to get to know people of different races. They both will never forget their first bus ride.

"I am proud to be a small part of something so important and grateful to the community who fought hard to make it possible for us to learn together as equals."

• **Monica Lash**

"I feel fortunate to have been a small part of the pairing program. We learned so much from each other as equals that had been denied to many before us."

• **Molly Johnson**

Mr. Andrews worked at Field School from 1971 to 1989 and also lived in the Field neighborhood.

"What you are going to be you are now becoming"

• **Mike Andrews**

Heidi Adelsman & Mr. Andrews, 2017

Heidi Adelsman was in 5th grade in the Green Unit with Mr. Andrews former teacher, principal, coach and community leader, in 1971.

Heidi has collected oral histories, written and helped organize community events on desegregation since 2004, the 50th anniversary of the landmark supreme court's Brown vs Board of Education decision.

"*All of our schools should be good enough to attract a healthy racial mix, which, I believe, leads to the most effective learning for everybody.*"

• **Ruby Bridges**

DISCUSSION STARTER

- Why do you think people wanted to do the Hale-Field Pairing?
- When do you remember having your first friend that has a different background than you?
- What is one way you can get to know someone of a different background?

KEY VOCABULARY

Brown vs. The Board of Education

A decision made by the United States Supreme Court that said all children should be able to go to school together, no matter the color of their skin.

Segregation

Racial separation; it means keeping people apart because of things like the color of their skin, which is unfair and hurtful.

Integration

Ending racial separation; which means everyone gets to learn and be together, making schools fair and welcoming for all children.

Hale-Field Pairing

An integration plan by Minneapolis Public Schools to merge Hale and Field Elementary.

LESSON PLAN QR CODE

Learn more at: www.separatenotequalmn.org

ABOUT THE AUTHOR

Derek Francis is an educator, film producer and author that elevates creating welcoming, culturally responsive school environments for all students.

In 2024 Derek produced Separate Not Equal - Minnesota Integration Story which was selected for the Twin Cities Film Festival.

Derek has lead professional development at schools, communities and conferences nationally. He lives in Fridley, MN with his daughter Grace.

ABOUT THE ILLUSTRATOR

Ashley Finch is an illustrator who loves science fiction, horror, and history.

Since graduating from the College of Visual Arts, she has taught visual art to children and adults, and created illustrations for a variety of projects.

Her work has been shown both nationally and internationally. She lives in Saint Paul, Minnesota with her family and a clowder of adorable (yet at times troublesome) cats.

www.ingramcontent.com/pod-product-compliance
Ingram Content Group UK Ltd.
Pitfield, Milton Keynes, MK11 3LW, UK
UKHW060120010826
14089UKWH00005B/78

9 781948 529266